Disclaimer

The subjects in this book are about my life. In no way am I telling anyone to commit any crimes whatsoever! This book is to entertain you!

Happy reading...

Chapter 1
Economics 101

You may have thought economics was just a business class but it is much more than that. Economics is a behavioral science. It can be defined in four words, HUMAN ACTION UNDER SCARCITY. Here is some basic economics I think you should know before we get started.

Economy
A system in which scarce resources are allocated among competing uses.

TANSTAAFL
There **ain't no** such **thing as a** free lunch

FREE MARKET
A system in which the prices for goods and services are determined by the open market and consumers, the laws and forces of supply and demand are free from any intervention by a government, price-setting monopoly, or other authority.

5 Characteristics of a Free Market System

1. Private Property. People own stuff, not the government.

2. Freedom of Choice. Everyone can choose what to do/buy/sell.

3. Motivation of Self Interest. People do things that benefit themselves.

4. Competition. Sellers have a competitive drive, thus better quality, more variety and lower prices.

5. Fuck Government. The people decide stuff, not the government.

BLACK MARKET

The illegal buying and selling of goods above the price fixed by a government. Black Markets usually develop when, because of war, disaster, or public policy, a government tries to set prices for commodities instead of allowing the normal operations of supply and demand to set prices.

The black market is also the venue where highly controlled substances or products such as drugs and guns are illegally traded.

The Self-Organizing Economy

The greatest insight of economists is that an economy based on free-market transactions is self-organizing. That means there's no need for any fucking government, or any dumb ass institution to tell us what to sell, what to buy, and what to trade. Let the laws of supply and demand determine how the economy is to operate.

Main Characteristics of Market Economies

Here are the main characteristics of market economies that produce this spontaneous self-organization.

Self-interest. People buy and sell what seems best for themselves and their families.

Incentives. Sellers want to sell more when prices are high, and buyers want to buy more when prices are low.

Market prices and quantities. The price of goods and the quantity of goods sold are determined in free markets in which would-be sellers compete to sell their products to would-be buyers.

Resources (3 Broad Categories):

1. Land
2. Labor
3. Capital

Land

All natural endowments such as arable land, forests, lakes, and minerals.

Labor

All human resources, both mental and physical.

Capital

All manufactured aids to production such as tools, machinery, and buildings.

Factors of Production

Resources used to produce goods and services; frequently divided into the basic categories of land labor and capital.

Goods

Tangible commodities, such as cars and shoes.

Services

Intangible commodities, such as haircuts or medical care.

Production

The act of making goods or services.

Consumption

The act of using goods or services to satisfy wants.

Scarcity and Choice

Scarcity implies that choices gotta be made and making choices implies the existence of costs.

Opportunity Cost

The cost of using resources for a certain purpose measured by the benefit given up by not using them in their best alternative use. Every time a choice is made, opportunity costs are incurred.

4 Key Economic Problems

1. What is produced and how?
2. What is consumed and by whom?
3. Why are resources sometimes idle?
4. Is productive capacity growing?

Specialization

People's abilities differ, and specialization allows each

person to do what he or she does relatively while leaving all the other shit to be done by others.

Division of Labor

When the production process is broken up into a series of specialized tasks, each done by different workers.

Economic Systems (4x)

1. Traditional economies
2. Command economies
3. Free-market economy
4. Mixed economy

Traditional economy

An economy in which behavior is based mostly on tradition.

Command economy

An economy in which most economic decisions are made by a central planning authority.

Free-market economy

An economy in which most economic decisions are made by private households and firms.

Mixed economy

An economy in which some economic decisions are made by firms and households and some by the government.

I believe the free-market economic system is the best, the laws of supply and demand are able to function freely without any government intervention. This country calls our economic system the free-market but as you know the government intervenes constantly in the affairs of buyers and sellers. That is why the black market is the real free-market, the laws of supply and demand operate as they should without someone telling you what the fuck you can buy, sell, and trade.

Demand

Quantity Demanded

The amount of a good or service that consumers wish to purchase during some time period.

One, quantity demanded is a desired quantity.

Two, quantity demanded refers to a flow of purchases. Therefore, it must be expressed as so much per period of time: 500 units per day, 100,000 units per week, 1 million units per year.

Quantity demanded is influenced by the following variables:

- Product's own price
- Average income prices of other products
- Tastes
- Distribution of income
- Population
- Expectations about the future

Law of demand (stated 3 ways)

1. Price and quantity demanded are inversely related.
2. When the price of a product goes down people will buy more, and when the price of a product goes up people will buy a lot less.
3. The demand curve alway goes from the top left to the bottom right.

Law of demand

1. Price down - people buy more

2. Price up - people buy less

Supply

Quantity Supplied

The amount of a commodity that producers wish to sell during some time period.

One, quantity supplied is a flow; it is so much per unit of time.

Two, quantity supplied is the amount that producers are willing to offer for sale not necessarily the amount that they succeed in selling.

Quantity supplied is influenced by the following variables:

- Product's own price
- Prices of inputs
- Technology
- Government taxes or subsidies (not in black markets)
- Prices of other products
- Expectations about the future
- Number of suppliers

Law of Supply (stated 3 ways)

1. Price and quantity supplied are directly related.
2. When the price of a product goes up, suppliers will supply more, but when the price of a product goes down, suppliers will supply less.
3. The supply curve goes from the bottom left to the upper right.

Law of supply

1. Price goes up - suppliers supply more
2. Price goes down - suppliers supply less

Equilibrium

Economic equilibrium is a condition or state in which economic forces are balanced. ... Economic equilibrium may also be defined as the point at which supply equals demand for a product, with the equilibrium price existing where the hypothetical supply and demand curves intersect.

Chapter 2

CRACKANOMICS 101

The year was 1999 and I had just moved from Kent Ohio to Akron Ohio's Northside. When we moved over there it was fucking dangerous. I didn't have a job, no money, and no car. My cousin and I decided we were going to sell crack. I know it sounds crazy but we felt like we came up with the plan of the century. Our only problem was we didn't have any money to start with. In order to sell crack you have to know a dealer who will front you or you must have your own money and buy it from a connect (dope wholesaler).

We definitely didn't know anyone who would front us so we had to come up with our own money fast. Around the corner from my house was a temporary service that paid you each day you worked. So off we went to work hard as fuck for $40 a day. We worked for two weeks

 in some fucked up sweatshops. Some of them had to be

110 degrees in there. But after 2 weeks we finally each

had enough money to buy a quarter ounce of crack for

$250. A quarter ounce of crack weighs 7 grams. We

packaged it up into $20 units. Each unit weighs 2 tenths

of a gram, so you get 5 $20 units per gram. That means

we got 35 $20 units out of our first quarter ounce.

Without giving any deals that will be $700 in revenue

and a net profit of $450. That's not bad money

considering you can sell out in one day. We were

excited as hell! We felt like we were on our way to

getting rich.

We bought quarters for a few weeks while we started to

build a regular clientele. Now we had to step our game

up, but first we had to deal with some issues in order for

us to do business without being interrupted. The issues

that we had to address in this business: protection, target customers, staying undetected by our competition, and getting and maintaining more than one supplier.

Protection

No one in their right mind would consider conducting business in the streets without protection. That means fucking guns. So number one on our priority list was to get strapped. We even came up with creative hiding places so that we were never more that a few feet from our pistols even when we were posted on the block.

Target Customers

Now it's time to get down to business. Just like in any business you have to decide who are your target customers. This is one of the most important part of any start-up. Due to the experiences I've had in the game I decided that selling dope to the prostitutes would be the most lucrative. Just like us they to are in business. They are in a service business that is in high demand so they are very rarely out of money. When you are dealing with customers who work all week and are paying bills and maintaining a home they are working with limited funds. In the dope game you want money coming in constantly, every day at high volumes, not once or twice per week. A prostitute that's on the hustle for real might be good to spend between $300-$1000 per day. Seriously! The reason I say up to $1000 per day is because some of the hoes' got customers who smoke to. That means even more money in your pocket.

Staying under the competition's radar

Doing business exclusively with the prostitutes is also a good way of staying undetected by your competition. You can basically hide in plain sight. Example: one of them chicks call you and she wants $100 worth of crack. You pick her up on the "block". This is the same exact way the "johns" pick up the hoes when they paying for sex. To everyone watching it's business as usual for the hoe. So if you're from out of town, at first muthafuckas ain't gonna know what the fuck you're doing until you already got your money and your guns up.

Getting and maintaining more than one supplier

In the dope game it is very necessary to have more than one supplier. You never want to run out of dope. It's always when you're doing good that all of a sudden your connect says he's out, and he'll hit you up when it's all good again. Some suppliers will fuck up your flow on purpose in order to keep you below them. They know that dealers who sell "pieces"(small units or retail) to the fiends are making more money per ounce than they are. Example: if you are selling dope on the retail side and you buy an ounce for $1000, that is 28 grams of crack. That is a potential revenue of $2,800. Even if you do deals to your loyal customers and you make back $2,000, you have easily doubled your money and made $1000. And if you are doing deals like that you will sell out in a day no problem.

Your connect is selling his dope wholesale. He's probably making between $300-$500 per ounce, and that all depends on his supplier and how much he buys at once, or if he's just a middleman for someone else. Your connects realize that if you know what you're doing you can pass them up in no time. That is why some of them will purposely "run out" on occasion to keep you below them and if you only have that one connect you are dependent on them and that's how they want it.

Hey that's why they call it hustling. You gotta hustle the fiends and you gotta make sure you ain't getting hustled by your connects. It's fucked up but that's how the game goes.

Chapter 3

Compounding

Many hustlers are stuck in a make money-spend money cycle. They buy their packs, sell all the dope, and spend their money on cars, clothes, and jewelry. Not to mention the money they throw away at the bars, strip clubs, and smoking good weed. Hundreds of dollars passes through the average hustler's hands every single day and the money is spent on bullshit. When I sold dope I did the exact same shit. I would go to the mall and spend $700 on shoes and clothes, buy me some bomb ass weed which would run me another $60, and hit the club that night and spend another $200. That's almost $1000 in one fucking day. Not smart at all.

When I realized how much money I was throwing away I decided to change the way I did things.

I knew in order to truly play by our own rules we had to get our money up. Warren Buffett, the most famous stock investor of our day said something that always stuck in my head. He said "compound interest is like magic". This made me think, I have to figure out how to compound my muthafuckin money. This is when I came up with the 36 hour shift.

So this is how the 36 hour shift works. We hit the block hard as hell for you guessed it, 36 hours straight during which time we buy and sell crack. Everytime we buy and sell out, we reinvest every single penny we made from the package we bought before. Now that's compounding for real! That's how you get your money up and fast, thousands of dollars in 36 muthafuckin hours!

The 36 hour shift is so serious you have to prepare ahead of time. If you are a small time hustler you have to take a couple of days of good hustling to save enough money to grab you a decent package. You want to start out with the biggest size package you can. Then you have to package it all up at once. You need a digital scale to be exact with your weights. Never take it all with you at once. If for some reason you don't live near the area where you will be hustlin find you a stash spot to keep some of your work. You can also just take what you can handle carrying on you and when you sell out just catch a cab back near your house, tell the cabbie to wait for you, grab more work, and have the cab drop you back off at the block. I did this for about six months straight. Just be cautious. Make sure your cab isn't being followed and don't let the cab driver know where you live. Some of them are gangsta's to and they will set you up if they think you got a lot of money in your house. Or if they are just some straight up busters they may snitch.

You have to be smart and well prepared.

Next, let them hoes know that you are about to go on a 36-48 hour run with some good work! The 36 hour shift was created with them hoes in mind. When they are on the grind and smokin like a broke stove, demand is high and you have to keep up. For example, I knew a few of them hoes who made $500-$1000 per day but didn't have a cell phone. They didn't feel the need to take on an expense because their life revolved around crack. I'm sure that has changed a little these days. Your best customers are the hoes so you have to stay connected, if the don't already have one buy them a $20 cell phone. Make sure it has minutes on your 36 hour shifts. When you are ready to hit the block give your best money making customers a $20 unit of some strong shit to get them going then leave and wait on that phone to ring.

When you see that you are getting low on work hit your connect up so you can re-up without breaking your flow. You don't ever want to run out completely. That's why it's beneficial to have more than one supplier. After your 36 hour shift get you some good sleep. You may want to stay off the block for a while just in case your face was seen too often.

Chapter 4

DOPE AS A COMMODITY

Dope is a precious fucking commodity. The price for drugs go up and down the same way prices for stocks go up and down on wall street. As a matter of fact all markets operate the same; stocks, bonds, real estate, dope, etc.. The problem is that most of us that were in the game were slaves to the market. Slaves to the market's buying and selling price the same way the average retail stock investor is a slave to the ups and downs of the stock market. Now on the other hand you have stock investors who have accumulated great fortunes such as Warren Buffet. Have you ever asked the question, how are they more successful than the average investor? I'll tell you. They buy companies at discounted prices, usually when the market is down and they hold onto them until they can sell at a stupid huge price.

There's a way that the street level dealer can put this same investment strategy into action. The dealer is always in the business of buying and selling dope. That's what he does to survive. He buys the dope at today's wholesale price and then sells at today's retail price. His profit is usually pretty good but they are still a slave to the market. In my opinion they still make more money selling dope than the average retail stock investor makes buying and selling stocks.

Ok, here goes! The street level dealer will constantly be buying dope at the best wholesale/bulk price he can get, and then selling it at retail. They do this without ever investing for the future. Just like a successful stock investor they have to implement the buy and hold strategy. The buy and hold strategy for the dealer is going to be very different than for the stock investor, but it works the same nonetheless. This strategy for the stock investor may take years to implement, but in the dope game the market moves much faster, and will only take a few months. At the same time the dealer is buying/selling/profiting, he should also be buying/stashing. Here is why, every year, maybe even a couple times a year there's what is called a drought, also known as "drought season". A drought season is when the demand for dope is high but the supply is low. During the drought season anyone still holding some work will make a great deal of money because the price is now very high. I would say 50-

100% higher depending on quality and scarcity. The dealers who have not prepared for this high demand will be a slave to the market because they will have to pay the high prices or go out of business. Some of the low level dealers will have no choice and be forced out of business. I remember a time when I was paying $225 for a quarter ounce of crack, and then out of nowhere the drought hit and I was happy to find a supplier selling at $350, and it was always a half gram short. A brutal game but someone had to do it. A street level dealer can still make money selling dope even at these prices. For example, as you know a quarter ounce weighs 7 grams which can cost you $350 during a drought. A regulation $20 dollar rock that a dealer sells to crackheads weighs .2, or 2 tenth of a gram. But during the drought your $20 dollar rock is going to weigh .1, or 1 tenth of a gram. That's how you stay alive and you can still occasionally sell 2 for $30 or 3 for $50 to your very loyal crackheads.

Follow the steps below and go from street hustler to boss!!! It's so fucking simple!

PLAN IN ACTION
1. BUY/SELL/PROFIT AS USUAL
2. "BUY AND HOLD" A QUARTER OUNCE PER WEEK. THAT'S AN OUNCE PER MONTH
3. IF YOU DO THIS FOR 9 MONTHS YOU WILL HAVE A QUARTER OF A KILO WHEN THE DROUGHT HITS
4. GO FROM LOW LEVEL DEALER TO A BOSS

Chapter 5

PRISONOMICS

I am writing this chapter because going to prison it's just part of the game. Hopefully you don't have to go but you should always be prepared for the worst. Your first day in prison you will be nervous as hell, especially if it is your first time inside. It's OK to be nervous just as long as you don't act like a scared little bitch. Your adrenaline will be pumping, it's OK use it as energy. The other inmates will be asking you a shit load of questions such as: what's your name? where you from? what county did you get sentenced at? You don't have to act super antisocial but say as least as possible. Me personally I like one word answers. One word answers are perfect because you're communicating without talking to much. Doing too much talking can be perceived as a sign of weakness. It also gives the hustlers an opportunity to read you. Reading a person is a way of sizing someone up mentally. So use direct and to the point answers, no need for long conversations, because you don't even know these muthafuckas.

Quickly learn the rules of the rules of the institution. As soon as you get there you will be given a rule book. Take fifteen minutes and read through it. This is important so you can move normally through the prison population without getting harassed. For example, in the prison where I did my time you had to be wearing your prison blues with your shirt tucked in and your ID badge clipped to your collar and there was no way you were going to move around the prison if you weren't properly dressed. So soak it in fast and put it away for reference purposes.

Next you have to learn how to deal with the other inmates, this is called "Prison Politics". Knowing how to deal with the other inmates is going to be crucial to your survival in prison. You have to quickly learn: what you don't do, what you don't say, when to say excuse me, what not to do or say in an argument, and when fighting is necessary. For example, if you are into it with someone and you say something like: you a bitch, you a hoe, you on some bitch shit, you on some hoe shit, bitch ass shit, hoe ass shit; you better be ready to fight to the death! Calling someone a bitch or a hoe in the joint is a super huge insult. And if anyone calls you a bitch or a hoe in the joint, well that's one of those situations when you have no choice but to "get in the paint" and fight like a muthafucka. If you don't people will assume you are a hoe in the joint and they will treat you like one. Let me also say this, it doesn't matter if you win or lose, just as long as you fight! So don't be afraid to lose a fight, you must do whatever necessary to maintain your respect. It basically comes down to just treating everyone with respect and never let anyone disrespect you.

If for some reason you do get into an altercation with another inmate it's best to resolve the situation right there on the spot. Regardless if you have to resolve the situation verbally or with violence, you must resolve that shit on the spot. I've seen horrible things happen to people who thought they could talk shit to someone and walk away. I've seen a guy get stabbed with not one, but two pencils. I've seen a guy get hit in the head with a steel locker box and no he didn't even see it coming. I've also seen a guy get hit in the head with a lock in a sock while he was asleep. So resolve all disputes right there on the spot. Better to square up and get in a fist fight than to get hit when you ain't looking.

GET YOUR MIND RIGHT

Now it's time to get your mind ready for the whole prison experience. You gotta get your mind right! This is the next step to surviving long stays in prison. You're about to be living in very close quarters with criminals of all kinds; drug dealers, murderers, rapists, pimps, along with a bunch of intelligent white-collar criminals. Yeah, the worst of the worst. Don't let any of these jokers fool ya, they may seem cool but at any moment without any warning at all these men or women can turn into man eating sharks. So be careful, these sober criminals are like evil geniuses capable of the most ruthless acts imaginable! This is the reason prison is such a serious place because you don't know what's going to happen one minute to the next.

Well I hate procrastinating so let's get down to it. I know you heard people say that to be a well rounded individual you must develop mind, body, and spirit. Well you heard right. These people you're going to be housed with have been developing themselves during the many months and years they have been incarcerated which puts you at a major disadvantage because you are way behind in this game. They have been studying all forms of business including but not limited to micro and macro economics, psychology, warfare, fitness including boxing and martial arts, religion and spirituality. Those of you who have never been to prison or don't personally know anyone who has been to prison are probably wondering why are these criminals studying all this shit. Some of you may not even believe it. Well it's true they're studying all this and more. A lot of these people are smarter than the people that locked their ass up. I met a guy inside who was a "jailhouse lawyer". He was so damn smart at the law that he was getting years knocked off some of the other inmates sentences. For a fee of course. This guy G got a friend of mine home eight years early. My friend was caught in a car with a "kilo" of cocaine and a pound of weed. That's a lot of shit to get caught on the road with. Well G helped him file an appeal and this dude won! I couldn't believe it. The county my friend was sentenced at sent a sheriff to take him back to court and then they released him. About a week later I got a letter from him, he was back home with his family. Wow! That's the shit

I'm talking about, these individuals are turning themselves into experts in a various subjects. You thought they were dangerous before they went to prison, you ain't seen nothing yet. This guy G turned himself into a law expert. My friend had paid lawyers thousands of dollars to fight his case and they couldn't help him, but this self taught "jailhouse lawyer" gets him out for fifty bucks. Ha ha ha ha ha.

DEVELOPING YOUR MIND

The brain is just like any other muscle, you have to exercise it, and the more you do the faster it will get and the more it will be able to retain. So the first thing you have to do is start learning. And no I don't mean go to the prison library and get a "nice" book to sit around and read to get your mind off your situation. You better be studying shit that will turn your mind into a weapon: business, psychology, body language, negotiation, health and fitness, secret societies just to name a few. So stay away from all forms of fiction including comics, romance novels, and hood books. What the fuck are they gonna teach you?

Now think back to when you were in school. How many classes did you have? I had English, Social Studies, Science, Math, Spanish, and Gym. We skipped from subject to subject with no problem. You have to retrain your brain to go from subject to subject again like when we were in school. Don't worry it will come back to you very quickly.

In addition to your regular studies here is a list of books you should become very familiar with:

- The 48 Laws of Power

- The Art of Seduction

- The Art of War

- The 50th Law

- Pimpology

- The Wisdom of Psychopaths

Some of these books may be banned from the prison you're in but someone there has them believe me. When you learn the ropes ask around you'll find them. As for the books that are not banned but are not in the prison library most prisons have some kind of program where you can get books from outside libraries sent in for a limited time like a week or two. The prison I did my time at had a program called "The Friends of the Library". It was $5.00 a year to be a member. Money well spent.

DEVELOPING YOUR BODY

Developing your body is a must in prison. Not for the same reasons people do it for out in the free world, to look good, or just for health purposes, although working out for your health is a good reason. But in prison you workout with one main goal in mind, and that's to turn your body into a fucking weapon. It's not something you do just to pass some time, or to be able to flex some muscles at your visit. It's to turn your body into a weapon and fast. If you haven't been working out before you went to prison you better start. Now! For the first three weeks you should be walking 1-2 miles everyday and doing push-ups. You are exercising your heart with your daily walking and you are developing your upper body strength with you push-ups. After that you can introduce pull-ups, dips, forward bends, side to side toe touches and squats to your daily workout routine. This is a full body workout. Do this workout for another few weeks before you start lifting weights. You have to get your foundation strong before you start working out with weights. You should do approximately 200 reps of each exercise. One way of doing your sets are called "down sets". Example: if you are doing 20 downs, which you gotta start with at least 20, your first set is 20 reps, your second set is 19, your third set is 18, and so on all the way down to one. That's OK for when you're doing basic calisthenics but when you're doing pull-ups and dips it may take you several months to be able to do 20 downs. So for pull-ups and dips try for 10 sets of 3 good reps.

DEVELOPING SPIRIT

Now when I talk about developing your spirit, I do not mean reading your Bible. I do not mean reading your Kuran, or your Torah. I mean developing Your Inner Strength, the Force that exists inside you. This is the force inside of you that will help you survive. There are several ways to develop your spirit. A strict exercise regimen and working hard are ways to strengthening your spirit. Studying also helps to develop your spirit. Meditation is another good technique to strengthen your inner spirit.

There different ways to meditate, and all depends on your goals. So let's with a technique.

1. Regulate your breathing, breathe in for 4 seconds, then hold for 4 seconds, then breathe out for 4 seconds. Continue this breathing pattern throughout your entire meditation.

2. Begin to visualize a flame of fire. With each breath the fire should get hotter and bigger.

3. Talk to yourself and say things like I'm a killer, I'm all powerful, don't want to come out work me no one can outthink me the one can beat me I'm all powerful.

4. Only do this meditation for about 5 minutes at a time. This is not for relaxation and if you do it too long you make it too hyped up.

5. Do every morning and every night.

Chapter 6

EXIT STRATEGY

One thing is for sure, you won't be able to sell dope for long without getting hurt, killed, or jailed. So with this in mind you should have a sound exit strategy. If you have properly stayed under the radar by not getting caught, maybe even working a part-time job, there are ways to getting out of the game and starting a new life.

You have to ask yourself, what do I need to get out of the game? MONEY!!! You need a steady income.

As a hustler you will need a real income coming in, not a $9.00/hr job. I'm not saying anything bad about people who work $9.00/hr jobs, I'm just saying as a dealer you ain't gonna want to do that shit. A dealer is use to having a more passive income than someone who works forty hours a week. So let us explore some possible investments that will be necessary to make a successful exit out of the game.

Buying a franchise would be a great investment. I know a couple of people who done very well by investing in successful franchises. Starting a business from scratch is all good but some people would prefer to start a business by investing in a brand that is already well known. A well known brand is its own advertising. If you buy a Subway franchise everyone that passes by it will know what Subway is all about, they'll even know a lot of the food that they sell from the commercials that are always on tv. But on the other hand if you start a business such as Joe's Cosmic Subs, no one knows anything about it.

Investing in rental properties is another great tool for exiting the game. Again the old buy and hold strategy. You buy the property and you hold on to it, and rent it out, every month you get your money like clock work. A lot of people think that being a landlord is risky, but I have been shot at, beat up with bats, hit in the face with bricks, pistol whipped in an attempted robbery, ran off the road, so to me investing money in something that ain't gonna get mad and beat my ass doesn't seem risky. Investing in numerous rental properties is a great retirement strategy.

Land is another good investment. Buy/hold/sell/profit. There it is again. Land is a very valuable commodity because God ain't making any more of it. If you buy lots in up and coming communities someone is going to want to buy them.

Whatever you decide to do make sure you put the same effort in it as you put in the game. Remember these are also parts of the game, they're just the other side of it.

www.ingramcontent.com/pod-product-compliance
Lightning Source LLC
Chambersburg PA
CBHW071150220526
45468CB00003B/1015